# RADICAL WHOLENESS FIELD NOTES

## From Fragmentation to Coherence, From Fear to Love

*by*

**Holly Woods PhD**

LIVING PORTAL
PRESS

**Living Portal Press**
An imprint of Emergence Institute
Durango, Colorado, USA

www.livingportalpress.com

Living Portal™, WildCreator™, CosmoSync™, Sequence of Coherence™, and the Involutionary–Evolutionary Flywheel™ are trademarks of Holly Woods, PhD.

ISBN: 978-1-1970938-02-9

First Edition: 2026

Printed in the United States of America

Library of Congress Control Number: 2026911011

# Table of Contents

# Preface
## Why These Field Notes Exist

This book is written for those who sense that the human experience itself is being asked to reorganize, not through improvement, optimization, or transcendence, but through a deeper kind of return. What is being restored is not a lost state, but a lost capacity: the ability of a human system to function as a whole.

Without Radical Wholeness, coherence cannot stabilize. Without coherence, clarity fractures under pressure. Without clarity, Love becomes reactive, creativity becomes forced, and participation in a complex world becomes exhausting.

These Field Notes were not written to explain Radical Wholeness as an idea. They arose from living into coherence and noticing what changes when an inner system reorganizes. This work is shaped by both lived experience and decades of scientific study. The CosmoSync™ family of methods and the Sequence of Coherence™ came later—a reverse-engineered articulation of the pathway so others could learn to cultivate what I first had to discover.

Over the past few years, I have watched a consistent pattern unfold in myself, in long-term clients, and, now, very clearly, among Living Portal participants. As protective structures soften through relational familiarity, something reorganizes. Inner opposition dissolves. Energy redistributes. Coherence returns, not as a state to maintain, but as an emergent property of a whole system.

This was not a surprise.

The return of coherence is an expected outcome of the work. Radical Wholeness operates along a clear involutionary–evolutionary trajectory: fragmentation gives rise to protection; protection distorts when it outlives its purpose. Essence is reclaimed through relationship, and energy is reassigned in service of wholeness. From this reorganization, coherence stabilizes. From coherence, alignment becomes reliable. And over time, the way life meets you begins to change.

These essays are Field Notes because they are written from inside that witnessing.

The Field Notes are not instructions, nor do they offer techniques. They do not attempt to summarize the CosmoSync™ methods or the full Sequence of Coherence™. That work lives elsewhere, in the *Radical Wholeness Primer* and in the Living Portal Initiation itself.

Instead, these Field Notes document what becomes visible as Radical Wholeness unfolds.

They name the felt shifts people experience when protection releases and effort decreases. They trace how exhaustion gives way to ease, how clarity emerges without force, how Love stabilizes without self-erasure, and how creativity becomes sourced rather than driven. They explore how coherence changes how we meet uncertainty and how, in turn, life begins to meet us differently.

This is not self-improvement; it is structural reorganization. And it matters deeply in the times we are living in.

We are facing conditions that continuously pressure fragmentation: acceleration, polarization, fear, and instability. Regulation helps us survive these conditions. Radical wholeness allows us to participate in them without becoming another fragment of the crisis.

These Field Notes are offered as a companion to the *Radical Wholeness Primer*, not a simplification of it. They are meant to be lived with, recognized in experience, and read in any order. Each essay stands alone, but together they trace a visible path: from fragmentation to wholeness; from effort to participation, from protection to Love.

If you recognize yourself in these pages, it is not because you are broken. It is because something in you is ready to reorganize.

Radical Wholeness does not ask you to become someone else. It allows you to become whole enough to trust yourself as you are.

What follows in the Author's Note offers brief context for readers who want it. It is not required for entry.

# Author's Note

This volume is part of a larger body of work published by Living Portal Press, the publishing home for writings that explore the evolution of human consciousness through Love.

*Radical Wholeness Field Notes* are intentionally observational, arising from lived contact with a coherence-first lineage rather than from instruction or method. They record lived moments, interior shifts, and recognitions that often accompany the stabilization of coherence, without attempting to explain or instruct.

These Field Notes are not meant to be read quickly or applied as practices. They are best met slowly, with attention to what resonates, what unsettles, and what asks for pause. Nothing here needs to be done. Recognition itself reorganizes. Readers are invited to trust their own pacing, to step away when needed, and to return when contact feels available again.

For readers who want a more explicit articulation of the conceptual frame and developmental logic that inform these reflections, *The Radical Wholeness Primer* is available as a companion volume. The Primer offers articulation and orientation; these Field Notes offer proximity to lived experience. Neither is required to read the other.

Living Portal Press publishes works meant to be met with presence and discernment rather than consumed quickly. Readers are invited to engage these texts in whatever order or rhythm supports clarity, coherence, and contact with what is alive.

# Lineage & Language Note

This volume emerges from the same lineage of work as *The Radical Wholeness Primer* and the Living Portal Initiation. Certain terms referenced implicitly or occasionally throughout these Field Notes (including Radical Wholeness, Sequence of Coherence™, Parts, WildCreator™, and the field of Love) are explored more fully in the Primer and in the CosmoSync™ family of methods developed by the author.

Here, these terms are not defined or instructed. They appear only as they arise within lived experience. Trademark symbols are therefore used sparingly or not at all, in the service of preserving the immediacy and intimacy of the reflections. Readers interested in the underlying frameworks, developmental sequencing, or methodologies are invited to consult the *Primer* as a companion volume.

# Chapter 1
# Living in Uncertain Times Without Losing Coherence

*Why Fragmentation Amplifies Chaos*

If you feel unmoored right now, you're not imagining it. We are living in a period of genuine instability—political, ecological, economic, and cultural. Systems we had always been told were durable are revealing their fragility. Narratives that once offered orientation are unraveling. For many people, the future feels opaque, even foreclosed. The sense of living on shifting ground is not psychological; it's contextual.

What's striking, though, is how differently people are responding to the same conditions.

Some are reactive and overwhelmed, cycling between urgency and collapse. Others feel frozen or apathetic, unable to locate direction or motivation. And some, often quietly, are meeting the same uncertainty with steadiness, discernment, and an unexpected capacity to stay present and engaged without being consumed.

This difference is not explained by intelligence, education, moral clarity, or access to information.

What I am witnessing in myself, long-term clients, and increasingly in Living Portal participants, is that coherence is the determining factor.

It's not certainty or confidence I'm speaking about. And certainly not control.

It's coherence.

Before we go further, it's important to name what coherence is *not*, because the word is often used loosely. Coherence is not calm, and it is not the absence of fear or grief. It does not mean you know what to do next, or that life suddenly becomes manageable. It does not protect you from loss, complexity, or moral ambiguity.

Coherence is your internal organization.

When you are coherent, your attention, values, and actions are aligned rather than competing against one another. There is a sense of inner alignment, even when external conditions are unstable. You can feel fear without being ruled by it. You can take in difficult information without fragmenting. You may not know what will happen, but you know where you are standing.

When coherence is absent, the opposite is true.

Uncertainty becomes unbearable not because it is threatening, but because there is no stable inner ground to meet it. Attention scatters. One part of you wants to act immediately, another urges caution, another feels hopeless; another demands certainty before moving at all. Energy is consumed by internal negotiation long before it ever reaches the world.

This is fragmentation.

Most people don't experience fragmentation as a concept. They experience life as feeling harder than it should, as difficulty sustaining direction. As exhaustion that doesn't resolve with rest. As knowing what matters but being unable to live from it consistently, especially under pressure.

And this is important: fragmentation does not begin in adulthood.

Fragmentation occurs during the formative years as an instinctive response to childhood conditions that asked us to adapt before we had the support to integrate what we were being asked to carry.

As children, our psyches begin to fragment when we must respond to incompatible demands without sufficient nurturing or relational support to hold the whole of us together. We learn to comply when compliance is required, even when it conflicts with our inner desire, truth, or impulse. We learn to prioritize belonging over authenticity when belonging feels necessary for survival.

Many of us were rewarded for performative behavior over childlike spontaneity. You can feel the pattern in small moments that seemed harmless, but weren't neutral: being asked to sing, dance, or play an instrument for an adult's approval; being praised for being "good," "easy," or "impressive"; learning that your value increased when you performed, produced, or pleased. Productivity was often rewarded over coherence, and adaptation over truth.

Each adaptation is intelligent. Each response makes sense in its moment.

But over time, these adaptations don't naturally reintegrate. They become layers of an increasingly false identity. The inner life becomes organized around switching rather than coherence. Different priorities dominate in different moments. Different values come online under different pressures.

While this is manageable during stability, it becomes devastating in uncertain times.

What I am seeing now, across many lives, is that the chaos of our external environment amplifies our internal fragmentation. The more unstable the world becomes, the more divided people feel inside. Fear accelerates. Reactivity increases. People either over-function, trying to hold everything together through sheer effort, or collapse into paralysis and despair.

They often blame themselves for this, assuming they lack resilience, clarity, discipline, or purpose. People try to compensate by consuming more information, refining their beliefs, or pushing themselves to "do better."

But effort cannot substitute for coherence.

In fact, effort applied to a fragmented system often increases exhaustion. It asks a divided Self to carry even more responsibility, to hold itself together in conditions that already exceed its capacity.

This is where Radical Wholeness becomes not just relevant, but essential.

When I say Radical Wholeness, I don't mean a mindset shift or a better coping strategy. I mean restoring coherence by meeting the protective structures within us with intimate, relational familiarity so their rigidity softens, their essence is revealed, and that essence can become coherent with self.

This process is multidimensional: what fragments us is rarely only "personal psychology," but also inherited, ancestral, karmic, and field-level patterning that the system has been carrying as protection.

Radical Wholeness begins with a different premise: that coherence is original. That beneath fragmentation lies an inherent organizing intelligence capable of holding complexity without collapse. The work is not to manufacture coherence, but to remove the conditions that prevent it from operating.

When coherence begins to return, something subtle but decisive shifts.

People report feeling more anchored, even when nothing external has improved. Decisions don't necessarily become easier, but they become cleaner. Attention stabilizes. Energy is no longer consumed by constant inner negotiation. Love becomes more available, not as sentiment, but as the capacity to stay present with what is real.

This does not make uncertainty disappear. It makes it livable.

In times like these, coherence is not a luxury. It is what allows us to remain human, capable of discernment, ethical action, and deeper connection, without hardening or breaking apart.

These field notes arise from witnessing that return of coherence, again and again, in real lives under real pressure. What follows in this series is not a promise of certainty, but an exploration of what becomes possible when inner fragmentation no longer governs how we meet an uncertain world.

# Inquiries

- Where does uncertainty most destabilize you right now—emotionally, relationally, or in your capacity to act?
- What inner conflicts consume energy before you ever engage the world?
- What might become possible if coherence, rather than effort, were the ground from which you respond?

# Chapter 2
# What Fragmentation Actually Feels Like

*How Inner Division Weakens Clarity Under Pressure*

If fragmentation were obvious, most of us would have recognized it long ago. But fragmentation rarely announces itself as a problem. It develops quietly, early, and intelligently, woven into how we learn to survive, belong, and function in the world. By the time we're adults, it feels like *who we are*, not something that happened to us.

Most of us experience fragmentation not as a theory, but as a lived, and unconsciously aware pattern:

- *Wanting incompatible things at the same time.*

- *Responding differently depending on context, audience, or pressure.*

- *Knowing what matters, but struggling to live from it consistently.*

- *Feeling internally divided when decisions carry weight.*

In calm times, these contradictions can feel manageable. When uncertainty looms, they become exhausting.

To understand why, we must examine how fragmentation forms.

As children, we do not have the capacity to integrate complexity. When faced with conflicting emotional, relational, or environmental demands, we adapt by changing masks. Some aspects of us come forward to meet expectations. Others retreat, wait, or go quiet. We learn, often without conscious awareness, which expressions are safe, rewarded, or necessary.

This is not pathology; it's intelligence.

A child who learns to be responsible in a chaotic household is not broken. A child who suppresses emotional needs to stay connected is not failing. A child who becomes hyper-attuned to others' moods is not disordered.

These adaptations are survival mechanisms.

Over time, however, these adaptations solidify. They become internal orientations rather than situational responses. Different aspects of us take charge in different circumstances—at work, in intimacy, under stress, in leadership, in conflict. What began as flexibility becomes structure?

This is how fragmentation becomes an inner architecture.

Most of us carry this architecture forward unconsciously. We learn to switch between roles, moods, values, and strategies without ever relating them to one another. There is no shared inner center coordinating response. Instead, life becomes an ongoing act of internal negotiation.

Again, in stable times, this can work.

External structures - jobs, routines, social norms - help hold things together. Fragmentation is buffered by predictability. But when those external structures begin to fail, the inner divisions are exposed.

When the external structure loses predictability, a fragmented inner architecture loses its reference point. Attention scatters, fear accelerates, and competing internal agendas pull in opposing directions. Part of you demands immediate action, another urges restraint, another sinks toward hopelessness, while another demands certainty before anything can move at all. In those moments, you're not simply responding to what's happening around you; you're expending enormous energy managing yourself at the same time.

This is incoherence.

Incoherence is not confusion about facts. It is a lack of internal alignment. When fragmentation governs your inner life, energy is consumed before it ever reaches action. Decisions feel heavy. Direction slips away. Even when you care deeply, you may feel strangely ineffective.

What I see repeatedly, in clients, in Living Portal participants, and in my own life, is that people often blame themselves for this. They assume they lack clarity, resilience, discipline, or purpose. They try to compensate by thinking harder, gathering more information, or pushing themselves to "do better."

But effort applied to a fragmented system does not produce coherence. It produces strain.

This is where many well-intentioned growth and healing approaches inadvertently stall development. They help us understand fragmentation, manage it more compassionately, or work around it more skillfully, but they often leave fragmentation in place as the organizing principle.

When we haven't resolved the inner fracture and still perceive the need for protection, we believe someone still must be in charge, to monitor, and to be hypervigilant. Someone still has to keep things from falling apart.

That vigilance is exhausting.

At a certain point, fragmentation has done its job. The system has learned enough. It has stabilized enough. What it needs now is not more understanding, but a different way of organizing.

This is the threshold Radical Wholeness addresses.

Radical Wholeness is how fragmentation resolves, not by dismissing protective patterns, but by approaching them in relationship. The work invites a sustained intimacy with what has been protecting you, so protection can de-rigidify, the original essence beneath it can be reclaimed, and that essence can come into coherence with self. And because fragmentation often spans more than one layer of identity—somatic, ancestral, karmic, and field-based—Radical Wholeness must be able to meet the whole system, not only the story of this lifetime.

Radical Wholeness does not ask you to eliminate fragmentation, nor to "fix" your childhood, nor to resolve every karmic thread before life can move forward. It recognizes fragmentation as a developmental phase, one that eventually must be completed.

Completion does not happen through force. It happens when the conditions that require fragmentation are no longer present.

When internal opposition softens, when different aspects of you no longer need to compete for control, coherence begins to return.

This is not theoretical. It is observable.

Among Living Portal participants moving through the first pillar, I see the same early indicators repeatedly. People describe:

- *Less inner argument*

- *Less self-surveillance*

- *More stable attention*

- *A growing sense of internal agreement*

- *Reduced effort just to stay oriented*

They are still living in the same world. The uncertainty has not been resolved. And yet, they are more anchored, less reactive. They are better able to discern what matters and act accordingly.

This is what coherence makes possible.

Coherence does not erase fear or grief, make choices simple, or make outcomes predictable. But it does provide a stable inner ground from which complexity can be met without fragmentation.

Over time, coherence also changes how life responds. When inner architecture is aligned, choices land more accurately. Timing improves. Effort decreases while impact increases. Many people notice an increase in synchronicity, not as something magical, but as a natural consequence of being internally organized.

When you are coherent, you meet life wholly. And life meets you differently.

Fragmentation is not a diagnosis, nor a failure. It is not something to eradicate. It is a developmental adaptation that, in time, can give way to something more integrated, more reliable, and more humane.

In uncertain times, this shift is not optional. Fragmentation amplifies chaos. Coherence makes uncertainty livable.

The rest of this book traces what unfolds as coherence stabilizes, how exhaustion lifts, how identity loosens, and how life begins to organize itself around a deeper intelligence than effort or control.

# Inquiries

- Where do you notice internal contradiction draining energy before you ever engage the world?

- What adaptations helped you survive earlier in life, but now feel burdensome to maintain?

- What might change if your inner life were organized around coherence rather than negotiation?

# Chapter 3
# When Protection Becomes Distortion

*How Exhaustion Indicates a Change in Inner Organization*

If you're exhausted right now, it makes sense. We are living through prolonged instability - political volatility, ecological disruption, economic uncertainty - and a collective grief that has not had time to settle.

I want to start there, because the exhaustion people are feeling is real. And yet, beneath that very real strain, I'm noticing another layer of exhaustion that often goes unnamed. I've felt it myself. I've seen it in long-term clients. And now I'm seeing it clearly among Living Portal participants as Radical Wholeness begins to take root.

This exhaustion is not caused by the emergence of coherence. It's caused by inner protection continuing long after it's needed. Understanding that distinction changes everything. Protection is intelligent. It is how we survive.

For many of us, our protective instincts in childhood required us to learn early to adapt to inadequate contexts (to stay alert, manage our responses, and suppress certain needs.) The patterns themselves, and the Parts of us that had to fragment to codify these patterns, were not wrong or bad. The protective patterns were expressions of care for life. They allowed our human system to function under conditions that did not yet support wholeness. That in itself is Love, doing the best it can with what's available.

But protection formed in childhood is meant to be temporary.

When the conditions that created the need for protection change, and the protective patterns remain, energy begins to distort. What once preserved life now constrains it. What once helped us function is now draining us.

This is where a deeper exhaustion arises.

Not because you are failing to cope or doing something wrong. But because you are still organized around a form of holding that no longer matches who you are now.

A popular term for this is "burnout," and it is real. But burnout alone doesn't explain why exhaustion often persists even after workload is reduced, boundaries are set, or rest is taken.

What I'm witnessing has a different quality.

It feels like being compressed rather than overworked, and more like friction than depletion. Like a force was applied for too long.

This is the exhaustion of distortion.

Distortion happens when protective structures outlive their usefulness. The system continues to brace, monitor, and manage even though the original conditions have shifted. The holding becomes habitual, unconscious, and rigid. Energy that once flowed into life becomes locked into maintaining a structure that is no longer needed.

You can feel this in the body.

In the jaw that never quite releases. In the shoulders that stay lifted even at rest. In the constant inner narration, checking, recalibrating, preparing.

It's as if the system is trying to fit itself into a shape that no longer fits, like forcing a square peg into a round hole. Effort is required not because life is inherently hard, but because the organization is misaligned.

This is why even small amounts of coherence bring relief.

And it's important to be precise about what I mean by coherence here, because it's often misunderstood. The coherence I'm describing doesn't come from calming the nervous system or improving coping strategies alone. Regulation and resilience can stabilize a fragmented system, but they don't resolve fragmentation itself.

Radical Wholeness does.

Radical Wholeness works by restoring the whole human system through intimate, relational familiarity with protective structures, often experienced as Parts, across multiple dimensions of experience. As protection softens, internal opposition dissolves, and coherence reorganizes around self rather than defense.

Without Radical Wholeness, you must actively manage coherence. As you become more whole, coherence stabilizes on its own.

When coherence begins to return, the load decreases almost immediately. Rigid identities soften, and inner constrictions loosen. The constant effort required to hold yourself together diminishes.

I've felt this myself, and many participants describe it in remarkably similar ways: a palpable moment when something inside finally settles and clicks into place. The body exhales. Tension that had been quietly held releases. It's as if a gear that's been slipping suddenly engages, and movement becomes smooth again. Less force is required. Less willpower. Life begins to move through the system rather than being pushed through it.

This is not a collapse or giving up. It's a reassignment. The energy that once went into bracing, monitoring, and self-protection becomes available again as creative life force.

Among Living Portal participants moving through the first pillar of Radical Wholeness, this shift shows up in consistent ways. People describe feeling more at ease even as their lives remain complex. They report less internal criticism or self-management, and less effort required just to stay oriented.

They're not disengaging from the world. In fact, most people who give up protective structures and begin to experience inner coherence become more present. They're more capable of staying with difficult conversations and less reactive under pressure.

It's not so much that they are less tired because life has become easier. They are less exhausted because distortion has begun to release.

Importantly, soul essence, the original life force beneath protection, begins to re-emerge. Qualities that were once bound up in survival become available for creativity, relationships, and meaning. Strength softens into presence. Vigilance becomes discernment. Control gives way to trust.

Nothing is discarded.

Protective patterns are not eliminated. They are repurposed. The intelligence that once kept you safe begins to serve alignment. The capacity that once held everything together becomes available for Love, contribution, and ethical action.

And this repurposing doesn't happen by telling protection it's obsolete. It happens through a relationship. Through intimate familiarity with the protective stance until its rigidity softens, distortion releases, and the deeper essence of that part can be reclaimed.

In Radical Wholeness, protective structures aren't pushed away. They're welcomed, loved, and transmuted, so the whole system can reorganize around Self rather than around defense.

Over time, as coherence deepens, people often notice a quiet shift in how life responds. Choices seem to land with less friction. Timing feels cleaner, less rushed or delayed. There is less wasted effort, fewer false starts, and a growing sense of moving with the current rather than against it. Synchronicity increases, not as a mystical reward, but as the natural consequence of alignment.

When you meet life holistically, life meets you differently. When we are experiencing internal instability, this transition matters profoundly. The temptation in chaos is to grip harder, to believe that effort is the only thing standing between order and collapse.

What I'm witnessing is the opposite. It's coherence, not force, that allows us to remain steady, ethical, and engaged without burning out or fragmenting further. So, if you're exhausted, it may not mean you need to try harder.

It may be a sign that protection has completed its work and that coherence is ready to lead.

# Inquiries

- Where are you still holding yourself together in ways that once helped, but now feel constraining?

- Which protective patterns continue more out of habit than necessity?

- What might change if you trusted coherence to reorganize your energy instead of forcing yourself to keep going?

# Chapter 4
# What Radical Wholeness Makes Possible

*Coherence, Love, and the Capacity to Meet the World*

When people begin to experience more ease, clarity, or stability in their lives, it's common to assume they've simply become better regulated.

They're less reactive, calmer under pressure, and respond more thoughtfully. In a culture saturated with nervous-system language, this is often where the explanation stops.

But what I'm witnessing, again and again in my own life, in long-term clients, and now very clearly among Living Portal participants, is that something more fundamental is happening.

The coherence I'm describing in these Field Notes does not arise because people have learned to cope better with fragmentation.

It arises because fragmentation itself is resolving.

That distinction matters.

Regulation can ease the surface of fragmentation and make life more manageable. Radical Wholeness changes the root organization.

Radical Wholeness restores coherence through intimate, relational familiarity with the protective structures within us, often felt as Parts. Rather than being confronted or overridden, they are met slowly, with attention and care. As this familiarity deepens, rigidity softens. Tension releases. The original life force held inside protection becomes accessible again, and that essence naturally comes into coherence with the self. Nothing is discarded. What once protected is welcomed home, repurposed, and allowed to serve life rather than defend against it.

The coherence described in these Field Notes is not something you maintain through vigilance or skill. Instead, it is something more unconscious: stabilization as the system reorganizes through a precise, multidimensional sequence of coherence.

Radical Wholeness names the moment when the human system no longer needs to organize itself around internal division, when protection has completed its work, distortion releases, and a single organizing center resumes its role.

Only then does coherence become stable.

Thus, coherence is not the starting point of this work. It is the result.

When Radical Wholeness begins to stabilize, people often expect dramatic change. What they encounter instead is relief. Relief from inner argument and constant self-monitoring. Relief from the effort of holding incompatible protective strategies together.

Many people say some version of the same thing: "I didn't realize how much I was managing until I stopped managing."

That relief is not psychological. It is structural.

When fragmentation resolves, the system no longer requires vigilance to stay intact. Attention stabilizes without force. Energy reorganizes itself. Identity loosens, not into chaos, but into coherence.

This is where true stability begins.

Stability does not mean predictability or emotional neutrality. It means the system can experience disturbance without reorganizing around defense. Emotions move through rather than taking over. Fear, grief, and anger no longer fracture attention because internal opposition is no longer amplifying them.

While fragmentation persists, we cannot cultivate inner peace. Such peace emerges only when fragmentation ends.

From this stability, clarity begins to arise, not as a product of analysis or certainty, but as a felt sense of alignment. Decisions land with less friction. Values no longer need to be argued into place. Action emerges without the same internal debate or need for justification, guided by an intelligence that is already whole.

This is not impulsivity; instead, it is discernment that no longer must compete with itself.

What Radical Wholeness removes is not complexity, but the inner conflict that once fractured attention. What remains is an ability to meet complexity without being pulled apart by it.

This shift becomes especially visible in relationships.

One of the clearest indicators that Radical Wholeness has stabilized is a qualitative change in how Love operates.

Without Radical Wholeness, Love is inevitably entangled with survival strategies: people-pleasing, control, withdrawal, and over-giving. Not because you lack care, but because fragmentation hijacks connection. Love becomes fragile under pressure.

With Radical Wholeness, love no longer needs to compete with protection. You can stay present without abandoning yourself, set boundaries without hardening, and remain connected without losing coherence.

Conflict no longer destabilizes who you know yourself to be. You can remain stable in your truth without needing to defend yourself. Love itself becomes more reliable and less reactive because your internal structures are more relational and compassionate.

This is why Love requires Radical Wholeness to last.

Another shift follows naturally: connection without entanglement.

As internal divisions resolve, people often report feeling more connected, not only to others, but to life itself. This is not fusion or loss of self. It is participation without distortion.

When you are no longer divided inside, you can belong without disappearing.

And then something subtle but unmistakable begins to occur. Life starts to respond differently. This is not mystical; it's what happens when inner architecture is whole.

When inner life is coherent because fragmentation has resolved, choices land more accurately. Timing improves. Effort decreases while impact increases. There are fewer false starts or misaligned commitments, and fewer situations that require constant correction.

What many people call synchronicity begins to appear here, not as a reward for being spiritually adept, but as the natural consequence of internal alignment and coherence. When your inner architecture is whole, actions arise from the same intelligence that is shaping the field you are moving within. Less effort is spent forcing outcomes. More becomes available to meet.

Radical Wholeness is not a lofty ideal. It is a practical necessity.

In uncertain times, regulation helps us survive. Radical Wholeness allows us to participate without fragmenting. We do not just need calmer humans. We need coherent ones, people whose inner lives are no longer divided, whose actions arise from alignment rather than urgency, and whose Love can withstand pressure without distortion.

# Inquiries

- Where has regulation helped you cope, but not resolved inner conflict?
- What changes when coherence arises from wholeness rather than effort?
- How does your capacity for Love, clarity, or ethical action shift as internal opposition softens?

# Chapter 5
# Love That Doesn't Fracture Under Pressure

*How Radical Wholeness Restores Love's Capacity*

Love changed for me when I stopped trying to protect myself from it. For a long time, I felt Love was something you earned, managed, or risked. Something that could be lost if you misstepped, gave too much, trusted too freely, or revealed the wrong thing at the wrong time. I thought Love was beautiful, but fragile. I thought it required strategy.

Then I began reclaiming Parts through the work of Radical Wholeness, and something I did not expect began to unfold. I started to experience self-love in a way that felt entirely unfamiliar, not as affirmation or self-improvement, but as a stable presence that was already there. It did not need to be convinced. It did not need to be performed. It did not disappear when I was messy, afraid, or uncertain.

That experience rearranged my understanding of what Love is.

Most of us care deeply. Most of us genuinely want to love well. We learn the language of Love early: romantic Love, familial Love, spiritual Love, unconditional Love. We speak of loving deeply, loving bravely, loving without conditions.

And yet Love is one of the most fragile capacities we have. It collapses under pressure. It distorts in conflict. It disappears when fear takes over.

This is not because people lack sincerity or devotion. It's because Love is not just a feeling or an intention. Love is a capacity, and like any capacity, it depends on how the human system carrying it is organized.

What I have witnessed, in my own life, in decades of client work, and now very clearly among Living Portal participants, is that Love does not reliably endure complexity, difference, or uncertainty unless the system itself is radically whole.

Without Radical Wholeness, Love is constantly hijacked by the need for protection. To see why, we must look beyond the stories we tell about Love and examine the structure that sustains it.

Most of us try to love from within a fragmented inner world.

Protective structures, our shields, if you will, are often experienced as Parts, taking shape early in life to help us survive, belong, and stay connected. Some Parts shield through pleasing. Others through control, withdrawal, vigilance, intellectualization, or self-sacrifice. Each part carries a form of care, but that care is shaped by fear, history, and adaptation.

These protective structures do not disappear simply because we enter relationships. They come with us.

When Love is attempted from within fragmentation, Parts compete for authority. Longing, fear, reassurance, and vigilance all pull at once, and Love becomes an arena where protection is constantly activated.

You manage yourself in a relationship: monitoring what you say, negotiating internally before responding, or overriding one impulse to keep another from being triggered. Even when there is real affection, something inside you is working very hard to keep things from falling apart.

I see this routinely. People are not failing at Love. They are working too hard at it.

This is not a moral failure. It is a structural one.

Without Radical Wholeness, Love requires ongoing effort because internal opposition remains unresolved. Protection remains rigid. Soul essence remains bound. The Parts that carry Love are filtered through survival strategies rather than sourced from wholeness.

Regulation helps here. Attachment skills can help. Communication practices can help. They stabilize the system and reduce harm.

But they do not resolve the underlying fragmentation.

This is where it becomes important to be precise about what I mean by Radical Wholeness.

Radical Wholeness is not simply "being more integrated," and it is Each Part work confined to one lifetime story. It is the restoration of the whole human system across multiple dimensions: somatic, psychological, ancestral, karmic, and field-based layers, through a precise Sequence of Coherence™. That sequence builds intimate, relational familiarity with protective structures, often experienced as Parts, not to dismiss them, but to soften their grip, reclaim their essence, and allow coherence to reorganize around self.

What becomes possible in radically whole Love is not more effort or control, but trust, because the system itself is no longer divided.

Rather than asking Parts to behave better in a relationship, this work invites intimate, relational familiarity with the protective structures themselves. Their rigidity softens, essence becomes available, and coherence reorganizes from within.

Nothing is discarded.

Protective structures are not bypassed or corrected. They are met, understood, and loved, often for the first time. As their protective stance de-rigidifies, the original life force they carry becomes available for something else.

This is the turning point.

When Parts are no longer organizing around protection, love no longer must compete with fear. That doesn't mean fear disappears. It means fear no longer runs the system.

From Radical Wholeness, Love arises from coherence rather than negotiation. Care no longer requires override or self-abandonment, and boundaries can be held without armor. Connection no longer asks you to leave yourself behind.

Love becomes stable. This stability is subtle, but unmistakable.

People tell me they can stay present in difficult conversations without dissociating or escalating. They can feel hurt without retaliating. They can speak truth without bracing for collapse. They can remain connected even when disagreements or differences arise.

This is not emotional suppression. It is integration. Because the system is now unified, Love isn't easily broken by stress. To reiterate my previous point: this is why Radical Wholeness is crucial for Love to endure.

Without it, Love is always vulnerable to regression. Under pressure, Parts revert to survival roles. Old dynamics resurface. Connection fractures, not because Love wasn't real, but because the structure carrying it could not hold the weight.

With Radical Wholeness, something else becomes possible. Love is no longer something you do. It becomes something you can sustain.

This also changes how Love relates to autonomy.

In fragmented systems love often requires a compromise of Self. People over-give, under-speak, or contort themselves to preserve connection. Boundaries feel threatening because they activate Parts that learned early that love is conditional.

From Radical Wholeness, autonomy and connection are no longer opposites.

Because the system is coherent, you can remain in a relationship. You can say no without panic. You can receive care without collapsing into dependency. You can allow for differences without needing to defend your identity.

This is Love without self-erasure.

Another shift follows naturally.

As Radical Wholeness stabilizes, Love often becomes less personal and more field-responsive. Care extends beyond familiar roles and relationships. People find they can stay open in the face of complexity, disagreement, even conflict, without closing their hearts or hardening into ideology.

This is not sentimentality. It is a strength.

Love, in this sense, is the capacity to remain open, coherent, and ethically responsive in a world that is unstable and often painful.

And this matters because we are living in times that will test Love relentlessly.

Without Radical Wholeness love, becomes brittle under the weight of fear, ideology, and polarization. People harden. They retreat into righteousness or despair. They confuse protection with integrity.

With Radical Wholeness, Love becomes a reliable presence. One that can hold differences without dehumanization, act without hatred, and set boundaries without contempt.

This is not idealism. It is a developmental necessity.

We do not need more people who believe in Love. We need people whose inner systems are whole enough to carry it.

Radical Wholeness is what makes that possible.

It allows Love to move through you without being distorted by fear, history, or fragmentation. It allows Love to meet uncertainty without disappearing. It allows Love to last.

# Inquiries

- Where has Love in your life been strained by protection rather than lack of care?

- Which protective Parts step in most quickly when the connection feels at risk?

- What might change if Love were arising from wholeness rather than effort?

# Chapter 6
# When Life Begins to Respond

*How Coherence Reorganizes Relationship with the World*

The first shift in moving toward Radical Wholeness is not that life responds differently.

It's that *you* do.

I want to start here, because this distinction matters. When Radical Wholeness begins to stabilize, people often describe it as if the world suddenly becomes more supportive or aligned. But what I'm seeing, repeatedly, is something subtler and more foundational.

You meet life differently because you are no longer divided inside. I noticed this in myself first, long before I had language for it. Then I began to see it clearly in clients. And now, I'm witnessing it very distinctly among Living Portal participants as Radical Wholeness takes root.

People don't suddenly become lucky, nor do they avoid uncertainty or hardship. What changes is their inner attitude.

They are no longer bracing themselves against experience or pushing themselves into action from fear or fragmentation. Because of this, they are better able to meet the moment. This is what Radical Wholeness makes possible.

When I use the term *Radical Wholeness* here, I'm naming the restoration of the whole human system across multiple dimensions, including somatic, psychological, ancestral, karmic, and field-based layers, through a precise Sequence of Coherence. As protective structures soften through intimate relational familiarity, coherence reorganizes around the Self. The result is not transcendence or control, but a system that can meet life without distortion.

From that wholeness, internal coherence begins to stabilize.

Internal coherence means your inner signals are no longer competing. You are not pulled in five directions at once, or saying yes while bracing for the consequences. You are not acting from one place while protecting against another.

You feel more congruent, your timing improves, and your attention stabilizes. And because of that, *your response to life changes*.

You listen more carefully and pause instead of rushing. You sense into what's emerging rather than forcing outcomes.

This is not passivity; it's accuracy.

From internal coherence, another aspect opens up: external coherence.

The world doesn't need to be orderly or predictable to achieve external coherence. External coherence occurs when the quality of your interaction with the field changes. When you are no longer broadcasting mixed signals through fear, urgency, or self-contradiction, your actions carry a different kind of clarity.

You make cleaner choices, recognizing invitations rather than chasing possibilities. You stop forcing doors that were never meant to open.

This is where many people notice that life feels less resistant.

I hear this most clearly when people say some version of, *"I didn't realize how hard I was pushing until I stopped."* That effort had become so familiar it was invisible. When protective structures are resolved, and internal coherence begins to stabilize, that constant pressure relaxes. Not because life suddenly becomes easy, but because you're no longer trying to force yourself, or the world, to make room for an inner split.

And only *then* does what we often call synchronicity begin to appear.

I want to be very clear about this, because synchronicity is often misunderstood. It is not magic. It is not a reward for positive thinking. And it is not something you can manufacture through intention alone.

Synchronicity arises when internal and external coherence align.

When your inner life is organized, and your actions are aligned with it, the field responds in kind. The right conversation happens at the right moment. An opportunity appears that does not require contortion. Something falls away, and you realize you had been holding it together by effort.

This sequence matters. Radical Wholeness restores the system, which allows a reliable internal orientation to form. As coherence stabilizes, your response to what life throws at you changes. From there, external coherence emerges, and what we call synchronicity follows.

I see this pattern repeatedly now.

Participants describe feeling less driven and more guided, not in a mystical sense, but in a grounded one. They stop trying to prove they are on the right path. They stop narrating their lives in terms of success or failure. They become more responsive and less reactive.

Uncertainty doesn't disappear. But it no longer overwhelms the system.

Instead of triggering urgency or collapse, uncertainty sharpens attention. People stay present longer. They sense timing rather than rushing to achieve a resolution. Fear may still arise, but it no longer organizes the entire response.

This is what it looks like when coherence replaces protection.

There is also a humility that emerges here. People recognize they are not in control of life, but they are no longer at war with it either. They experience themselves as participants in a living field that responds to clarity, integrity, and presence.

Effort gives way to participation, not as an idea, but as a felt shift in how life is met.

I want to say this carefully: life does not become benevolent or easy at this stage. Loss still happens. Conflict still arises. Grief still visits. But you meet these moments without fragmenting.

You don't abandon yourself to survive or harden as a protective response. As a result, the quality of engagement changes. For this reason, Radical Wholeness is not just an inner project. It has consequences.

When enough internal coherence is present, you become a different kind of participant in the world. One who can sense timing and respond without domination. You can act without burning yourself out.

This is often the moment when people realize that what they thought was personal healing was, in fact, preparation to engage life without distortion. To offer something real. To meet a world in crisis without becoming another fragment of it.

When life begins to respond, it is not because you have mastered reality. It is because you have stopped fighting it from within.

# Inquiries

- Where do you notice yourself responding to life from coherence rather than protection?

- How does uncertainty feel different when you are no longer internally divided?

- What shifts when participation replaces effort?

# Chapter 7
# Creativity Without Forcing

*How Sourced Creation Emerges from Coherence*

I used to believe that creativity required effort. Not just commitment or care, but a kind of internal pressure. I thought you had to push through resistance, stay focused longer than felt natural, and override doubt or fatigue to make something real.

And for a while, that worked. It even looked successful from the outside.

I was very productive. I could deliver on just about any request. I made things happen by force of will. From the outside, it looked like capacity. Inside, it felt like holding my breath for long stretches of time.

This way of creating worked until it didn't. And when it stopped working, it didn't fail gently. My body began to register the cost before my mind could make sense of it. Exhaustion accumulated. Joy thinned out. What had once felt alive started to feel brittle, compulsive, and strangely urgent.

I kept pushing anyway, overriding signals that demanded rest or recalibration. I told myself this was what commitment looked like. And more than once, that approach nearly caused me to crash.

That was the moment I could no longer ignore: what I was calling productivity was being powered by fragmentation. Creativity tied to survival can produce a great deal, but it exacts a price. Eventually, the system either hardens or shuts down. Avoidance sets in. Or force doubles down.

That breakdown wasn't a failure of creativity. It was the beginning of a different inquiry.

I see this pattern everywhere: in artists, leaders, visionaries, and healers. In people who once felt deeply alive in their work and now feel subtly depleted by it.

What I've come to understand is that much of what we call creative block is not a lack of imagination or motivation.

It's fragmentation.

When your inner system is divided, creativity requires negotiation. One part wants to express, while another fears exposure. Vision and exhaustion pull in opposite directions.

Creating becomes effortful even when the desire is still alive. You talk yourself into starting, overriding hesitation, and bargaining with fatigue. Sometimes you succeed. But it costs you far more than it gives back.

Radical Wholeness changes this in ways that often surprise people.

As the system reorganizes through the Sequence of Coherence, creativity stops being something you extract from yourself. It becomes something that *moves through* you. It comes first as a trickle, then as a steadier stream. Over time, sourced creation becomes a way of life.

Not because you've become more inspired, but because the internal opposition that once distorted creative energy has softened.

Protective structures, often experienced as Parts, no longer need to interrupt expression in order to keep you safe. Their protective stance relaxes, essence is reclaimed, and intelligence becomes coherent with self.

And when that happens, creative energy no longer leaks through fear, urgency, or self-judgment.

This is usually when people say something like, *"I'm making things again, but it feels different."* They don't have to push to get started or dread the process. They're surprised by what's coming through them.

What's striking is not just that creativity returns, but how it feels. There's less strain. Less self-monitoring or attachment to outcome.

Creation becomes more responsive than driven. More curious than controlled. You listen for what wants to emerge instead of imposing a plan from the outset.

This is what I mean by sourced creation.

Not passivity. Not withdrawal. But creation that arises when fragmentation no longer separates you from the creative field itself. As wholeness stabilizes, the impulse to create no longer requires manufactured motivation. It is sourced from the same intelligence that is shaping reality, because you are no longer split from it.

From coherence, timing improves. You sense when to act and when to pause. You don't force ideas to completion before they're ready. You don't abandon them prematurely out of fear or impatience.

You begin working with the process rather than against it. This also changes your relationship to productivity.

Before Radical Wholeness, productivity often functions as proof of worth, relevance, or value. Creativity gets tangled with survival and identity, and the system learns to override itself in order to keep producing.

After Radical Wholeness, that pressure eases.

People tell me they create less compulsively and more faithfully. They don't need to justify their work in the same way. They're less driven by comparison or urgency. They're more willing to let something take the time it needs.

And paradoxically, more gets done. Not because they're hustling, but because energy is no longer being spent managing inner conflict.

There's also a deeper honesty that becomes available. From wholeness, you're more willing to tell the truth in your creative work. You stop editing yourself preemptively. You stop trying to anticipate how your work will be received. You allow complexity and nuance to remain intact.

This matters now, when simplification is rewarded, and complexity is often treated as a threat.

A fragmented system tends to simplify reality to cope with internal strain. It flattens complexity into certainty, slogans, or ideology. Creativity becomes either performative or defensive.

From Radical Wholeness, creativity can hold contradiction. It can speak from uncertainty without collapsing and offer something real without dominating or persuading.

This isn't only about art, or writing, or innovation. It's about how ideas, solutions, and futures come into being.

Sourced creation allows new forms to emerge that are fit for the world they're entering. There's something else here that's often misunderstood.

Creativity without forcing does not mean waiting until you feel healed or finished. It means you are no longer fighting yourself to create. You still show up. You still engage. But you do so without coercion.

There is a difference between discipline and domination, and you can feel it in the body.

From coherence, discipline softens into something closer to devotion. Effort is no longer an act of self-override, but a form of commitment that wraps itself around you. Like a cloak you want to stay inside of. Work stops taking from you and begins to feel like participation in something already alive.

This is another moment when you realize that what you thought was personal work was also preparation.

What's being formed here is a contribution that isn't shaped by fear. As wholeness returns, the work you engage in no longer mirrors the fragmentation it came from. Creation begins to nourish the system that carries it, rather than drawing from it until it's depleted.

Creativity, in this sense, is not self-expression alone. It's a relationship with a living field that responds to clarity, integrity, and presence.

When you are no longer divided, creation no longer needs to be forced. You become available to it. And over time, that availability doesn't stop with what you make. It begins to shape how you show up. Creation reorganizes first, and then something quieter follows: your presence itself begins to take on coherence.

# Inquiries

- Where does your creative process still rely on pressure rather than coherence?
- What changes when you stop negotiating with yourself to create?
- What wants to emerge when you let creativity move through you instead of pulling it out?

# Chapter 8
# When Creation Becomes the Beloved

*How Coherence Reorganizes Relationship and Devotion*

For many years, I assumed that the absence of connection with another person in my life meant something was missing. Not in a dramatic way. More as a quiet wondering that surfaced in the still hours, or when something beautiful happened, and there was no one there to witness it with me.

I had been single for ages. I dated on and off. I stayed open. And as time passed, something unexpected occurred. Instead of becoming more flexible about what I could tolerate, I became more precise. Not sharper or more defended, but clearer. I could often feel, very quickly, when a relational field would require me to fragment to remain inside it.

This was not a judgment of others. It was a recognition in my own body. My nervous system had learned what coherence felt like, and it no longer confused intensity, chemistry, or intermittent intimacy with safety. I could sense when a connection was present, but sustainment was not. I could sense closeness, but there was no shared field to hold what was opening.

In earlier years, I might have tried to negotiate that gap. I might have told myself it was good enough, or that I was asking for too much, or that safety would come with time. But Radical Wholeness changes the threshold for what the system can tolerate. When the inner world is no longer organized around protection, the body becomes less willing to enter structures that require self-override as the price of connection.

At the same time, something else was happening.

Creation itself was becoming increasingly alive in me, not as a project or an ambition, but as a daily relational presence. The work wanted my mornings. Ideas arrived with insistence. Writing moved through me with a sense of inevitability that felt less like effort and more like stewardship. I was not overwhelmed, but I was occupied in the deepest sense of the word. My field was reorganizing around what was emerging.

It took time to understand that these two things were not separate.

There are seasons in development when healing is the primary relationship. Much of my earlier aloneness belonged to that phase. Repairing internal trust. Reclaiming parts of myself that I had learned to stay hidden. Learning how to live without bracing. Those years were necessary, and they were not yet creative in the way I mean here.

This recognition came later, after coherence stabilized enough that Love no longer had to be negotiated internally. It is not the first threshold most people cross. I have seen hints of it in some long-term clients and am beginning to see early signals in a few Living Portal participants, but it is not common at the outset. It tends to arrive only when the system has become whole enough to stop organizing life around repair.

Once fragmentation resolves, Love reorganizes itself.

The question quietly shifts from who will meet me to what is asking to move through me. This is not a rejection of human companionship. It is a reordering of devotion. Creation becomes relational not because it replaces relationship, but because it meets a Self that no longer seeks completion through another.

Creation responds to coherence and deepens with presence. It withdraws from self-betrayal. It is exquisitely sensitive to how a life is organized. When creation is alive in this way, it is not a strain; instead, it flows. It asks for fidelity, clean attention, and honest pacing. It asks for a life that does not require constant internal negotiation to function.

In that context, making an intimate human connection central can be destabilizing.

Making our human relationships central is not wrong, but it often requires dividing attention, negotiating rhythm, and prioritizing reassurance over alignment. It invites subtle self-editing. It pulls the center away from the work being tended. A coherent system can feel that cost immediately, even when a person is kind, even when there is care, even when there is attraction.

This clarified something essential about intimacy for me.

Intimacy is not episodic. It is not something that turns on and off. It is a field condition. When relational structures lack containment, when there is no shared field to hold what opens, my body stays vigilant even if the connection is pleasurable. That vigilance is not fear. It is intelligence: the system protecting coherence itself.

I have learned that safety does not come from labels, proximity, or agreement. It comes from coherence. When coherence is stable, Love does not fracture as easily. When coherence is stable, creativity does not require forcing. And when coherence is stable, a life begins to organize around what is most true, rather than what is most familiar.

This has made companionship rarer and aloneness more frequent. That is not always easy. I still feel the ache of wanting someone nearby who can meet me at the depth I now live. But I no longer treat that ache as proof that something is wrong. I recognize it as a real human longing held inside a deeper fidelity.

In this season, creation has become beloved.

Not as an abstraction, but as a lived devotion. It meets me daily. It does not ask me to shrink. It does not require explanation. It does not pull me away from my center. It asks only that I remain available to what is already alive.

That human connection we think is missing will return when it can stand beside this without competing with it, when Love can be adjacent rather than central, when intimacy does not require me to reorganize my life away from coherence. When companionship can include devotion, rather than asking devotion to move aside.

Until then, I am not waiting.

I am tending.

And that, too, is a form of Love.

# Inquiries

- Where has coherence stabilized enough in you that love is reorganizing itself?

- What forms of connection ask you, subtly or explicitly, to fragment to belong?

- What does your system treat as "safe" now that you have tasted coherence, and what no longer qualifies?

- Where might creation be asking for fidelity rather than effort in your life?

- If devotion were reorganized around what is emerging through you, what would become simpler?

# Chapter 9
# Living as a Coherent Signal

*When Presence Becomes an Offering*

There comes a moment in this work when you realize that what you offer the world is no longer primarily what you *do*. It's how you *arrive*.

This often comes after creativity no longer requires force. When you are no longer extracting from yourself to make something happen, the way you enter a room begins to change.

I don't mean this poetically or in an aspirational sense, but very practically. As Radical Wholeness stabilizes and coherence becomes more consistent, people notice that their presence itself carries a different quality.

They're not trying to hold it or perform it, and they're no longer managing how they're perceived. They're simply there.

I noticed this in myself first, almost accidentally. My conversations changed tone, and my relationships slowed down. Difficult topics surfaced without escalation or urgency to resolve them. I didn't have better answers; there was simply less need to defend or fix.

Then I began to see it in clients. And now, very clearly, I'm seeing it among Living Portal participants.

When the inner system is no longer fragmented, presence becomes coherent. Coherent presence has an effect. This doesn't make you special; it makes you *available*.

In a fragmented world, most interactions are shaped by protective structures and habits. People brace before speaking. They simplify to be understood, or posture to be safe. Even care can feel strategic.

When you are internally divided, you can't help but contribute to this. Your nervous system broadcasts urgency or vigilance, even when your words are kind, and others respond to that signal instinctively.

From Radical Wholeness, that broadcast changes.

When protective structures have softened through relational familiarity, when coherence reorganizes around Self, your system stops sending mixed signals. You are not bracing against the moment. You are not rejecting what's arising within you in order to stay intact.

You can meet what's here. And that changes the interaction before a single word is spoken.

People often ask, "What am I supposed to do with this coherence?" They assume it needs to be expressed or consciously applied.

But one of the most surprising realizations is this: coherence is already doing something. It slows things down, invites honesty, and reduces reactivity without suppressing truth.

You don't have to persuade, or fix, or even lead. Your presence becomes a stabilizing reference point, not because you're calm or wise, but because you're not internally at war.

This is especially important in the times we're living in.

We're surrounded by fragmentation, polarization, fear, and an accelerated sense of urgency. People are overcome, overstimulated, and often operating from protective reflexes.

In that context, coherence is not passive. It's disruptive.

A coherent signal interrupts the feedback loop of escalation. It offers another rhythm or pace, another way of being with what's difficult.

I want to be clear here. Living as a coherent signal does not mean withdrawing from action or conflict. It doesn't mean being neutral or disengaged. And it certainly doesn't mean bypassing pain or injustice.

It means that your response arises from wholeness rather than defense.

You can name what's true without hardening, set boundaries without contempt, and stay human in situations that pressure you to fragment. This is not a role you adopt. It's a consequence of inner organization.

From coherence, you also notice when *not* to act.

This can be surprisingly difficult for people who are used to fixing, helping, or leading from a sense of urgency. But as coherence stabilizes, timing becomes more intelligible. You sense when intervention would be intrusive rather than supportive. You recognize when silence is not avoidance, but attunement.

Participation becomes more precise. And because of that, your actions land differently when they do arise - less reactive, less performative, less entangled with outcome. You're not trying to be heard. You're responding to what's happening.

This is one of the ways coherence contributes to the field without effort.

Another shift often follows.

As people live this way for a while, they begin to feel less alone. Not because they're constantly connected or affirmed, but because they're no longer exiled from themselves. There's an internal companionship that wasn't available before.

From that ground, being with others becomes simpler. You don't need to agree to stay connected or convince others that you belong. Nor do you need to disappear to keep the peace.

You can remain present in difference. This matters deeply right now.

A fragmented world does not need more certainty or louder voices. It needs people who can stay coherent under pressure, hold complexity without hardening into ideology, and remain in relationship without sacrificing truth.

Living as a coherent signal is not something you strive for. It emerges as Radical Wholeness takes root.

And it's humbling.

You realize that your contribution is not always visible or measurable. You may never know how your presence affected a conversation, a decision, or a moment of restraint. You may never see the downstream effects.

But you trust that coherence matters, even when it isn't credited.

This is quiet work. The work of being someone who does not add fragmentation to an already fragmented field. The work of meeting life and others, without splitting yourself to do so.

You don't have to announce it, or teach it, or prove it. You live it. And that is an offering.

And then the next question arrives: can this coherence hold when the world does not?

# Inquiries

- How does your presence change when you're not managing yourself internally?
- Where might coherence itself be the most honest contribution you can offer right now?
- What becomes possible when you trust presence as much as action?

# Chapter 10
# Staying Coherent in a World That Isn't

*Abiding Wholeness Without Withdrawal*

One of the questions people begin to ask as coherence stabilizes is not *how to deepen it*, but how to keep it, especially when the world does not slow down in response.

Not keep it in a possessive way, but more like a concern that comes from the earlier lived experience of being fragmented.

*"How do I stay coherent when the world is so chaotic? Can this wholeness actually hold under pressure?"*

These are honest questions. And they arise not from doubt, but from contact with reality. We are living in a world that is loud, polarized, accelerated, and often destabilizing. Fear and outrage are rewarded, and simplified narratives are favored over complexity or truth. Many environments are not designed to support coherence but to provoke a reaction.

So, it's natural to wonder whether Radical Wholeness is fragile in such conditions. What I've come to see is that coherence doesn't disappear under pressure. In fact, pressure reveals where coherence is still forming and where protection is still needed.

This is important to understand.

Radical Wholeness does not make you impermeable or lift you above the world. You still feel what's happening. You may still register threat, grief, anger, and confusion. You will encounter people who are reactive, defensive, or acting from fragmentation.

The difference is not that these things stop affecting you. The difference is that you no longer fragment *in response*.

Before this work, pressure often forced a split. You'd harden, collapse, over-function, withdraw, or disappear inside protection. You'd leave yourself to survive the moment.

From wholeness, something else becomes possible. You feel the pressure, but you stay here.

That staying is not passive, nor is it endurance or spiritual stoicism. Instead, it is the capacity to remain internally coherent while something difficult is happening around you.

I've watched clients or Living Portal participants encounter situations that would have completely destabilized them previously: conflict at work, family dynamics, collective fear, critical health issues, and uncertainty about the future. And while they still feel shaken, they don't lose themselves in the same way.

There is less escalation, less self-betrayal in the name of belonging, and far less pressure to contort oneself just to keep the peace. They remain present. This is one of the clearest signs that Radical Wholeness has taken root.

Staying coherent in a fragmented world does not require constant vigilance. In fact, vigilance often undermines coherence. What it requires is a system that no longer needs to be split to function.

As protective structures soften and their essence is reclaimed, the environment has less leverage over you. The impulse to armor against every stimulus eases. Difference no longer threatens your sense of integrity.

With more internal room, choices that once felt unavailable begin to open. You don't need to step away to avoid collapse. Staying engaged no longer requires being consumed. And when you need to speak your truth, you're not coming from the need to dominate.

And sometimes, you can simply refuse to participate in dynamics that require fragmentation as the price of entry. Refusal is quiet, but powerful. It doesn't look like disengagement. It looks like discernment.

One of the hardest things for people in this phase is realizing that not every situation deserves their coherence. Not every environment can meet it, nor is every battle worth entering. From wholeness, you begin to sense where your presence contributes, and where it would be eroded. This isn't selfish. It's responsible.

A coherent system cannot be sustained by repeatedly entering spaces that demand self-betrayal. And yet, Radical Wholeness doesn't lead to isolation either. It leads to *selective participation.*

You begin to choose where and how you show up.

This also changes how you relate to collective fear.

Fear still moves through the field, and you feel it without going numb. What changes is the compulsion to amplify it through reaction. Urgency no longer must be taken on as your own, and despair is no longer required as proof of care. Concern can be felt without being amplified, and grief can move without overwhelming the system.

You care because you're here. From coherence, care becomes steadier. Less performative or reactive. More capable of sustained response.

A world in crisis doesn't need more fragmented reactions, even when those reactions are well-intended. It needs people who can stay whole while witnessing what is breaking. People who can grieve without collapsing. People who can act without hatred.

Staying coherent in a fragmented world is not about avoiding impact; it's about remaining whole within it.

And that has consequences.

You become someone who inspires more rational thought just by presence; a pivotal figure who doesn't escalate, and who can hold complexity without simplifying it into ideology.

You don't fix the world by doing this. But you stop adding to the fracture.

This is quieter than most change narratives. It doesn't announce itself. It doesn't guarantee results. But it's real.

And over time, it reshapes how you live, relate, and contribute.

Radical Wholeness is not about escaping the world's instability. It's about meeting it without losing yourself. That may be one of the most needed capacities of our time.

# Inquiries

- Where does the world most pressure you to fragment to belong or be effective?
- What helps you stay present without hardening when things feel unstable?
- Where might selective participation be an act of coherence rather than withdrawal?

# **Chapter 11**
# Love, Creation, and Coherence as a Way of Life

*When Radical Wholeness Becomes Orientation*

At a certain point, this work stops feeling like work. Not because there is nothing left to tend, but because Radical Wholeness is no longer something you return to. It becomes how you're oriented.

For some, this also becomes a season when your relationship with others is decentered, not because Love is absent, but because devotion is reorganizing around what is being stewarded.

You don't wake up thinking, *"How do I stay coherent today?"* You wake up already inside a system that knows how to meet what arises, without rehearsal or bracing.

This is the quiet shift I'm seeing now: Love stabilizes, and creativity eases. Coherence no longer requires protection. Love and coherence seem to intertwine as a single way of being, rather than separate capacities you manage.

I didn't expect this when I first began this work. I thought Radical Wholeness would be something you achieved and then maintained, like a hard-won state you had to guard. What surprised me was how ordinary it became. Not flat or diminished. Ordinary in the sense that it no longer required constant attention.

Love is felt first as inner adequacy. A sense of being enough without effort or defense, and an ability to hold yourself with compassion even when things remain unfinished or uncertain. From that ground, creativity and coherence move naturally, without strain or announcement.

This is often the moment people realize they are no longer doing Radical Wholeness, but living from it. Love is no longer something to work on or manage, but something trusted, because the system carrying it is whole. Urgency, attachment, and self-erasure lose their hold, and Love becomes a stable ground for truth.

From that stability, honesty no longer hardens, and care no longer collapses. Connection doesn't require self-abandonment. This isn't the result of mastering relationships, but of no longer being divided against yourself.

Creativity no longer arrives in episodes. It's not something you get back to when conditions are right, or something you must push into being. It becomes the way you engage life, how you respond, experiment, and meet what's emerging.

Creation is no longer something you have to schedule. It becomes something you live with.

When fragmentation resolves across time, psyche, body, and field, the human system becomes whole enough to source creation again. Creativity is no longer generated through effort or received as inspiration but arises from direct participation in the same living intelligence that is already shaping reality.

Pressure gives way to participation. Creation moves through ordinary moments and consequential ones alike. You sense it in conversations and decisions, small gestures and bold experiments, quiet insights and innovations that reshape how things are done. Sometimes it's subtle, a timely word, a reframe, a choice not to escalate. Other times it carries real momentum, expressing itself as joyful creation, meaningful offerings, or work that ripples outward into the world.

This is sourced creation as a way of life, not episodic inspiration, but sustained participation in what is emerging, made possible by a system that is no longer fragmented from the source of creation itself.

Because your system is organized, you don't burn yourself out trying to be ethical, creative, or loving. You don't need to manage yourself into alignment or force integrity. Instead, you respond from alignment.

What becomes clear is that Radical Wholeness was never about becoming better. It was about becoming available. To love without distortion. To create without forcing. And to meet a world in flux without fragmenting.

This availability changes how you relate to time. You stop rushing toward outcomes. You no longer narrate your life as a project, and cease asking whether you're there yet.

Instead, you begin to live inside a rhythm that is responsive rather than reactive. This doesn't make life predictable. It causes life to be workable.

You know how to pause or act, and when waiting is the action. Not because you're certain, but because you're coherent.

One of the most moving things I'm witnessing among the Living Portal participants is how people are beginning to trust themselves again, not as personalities or identities, but as systems that can be relied upon.

They stop outsourcing authority to urgency, comparison, or fear. They no longer need external validation to know whether they're aligned. And they begin to sense when something is true for them, even when it's uncomfortable or unpopular.

This is what it means for Radical Wholeness to become orientation. It's no longer a response to fragmentation, but the ground from which life unfolds.

And importantly, this does not pull people away from the world. It brings them into it more honestly.

People become more discerning about where they invest energy, being selective about commitments. They are willing to say no when yes would require self-betrayal.

At the same time, they're often more generous and patient. More able to stay in the room when things get difficult.

This is not a contradiction. It's coherence.

Love, creation, and coherence stop competing for attention. They begin to reinforce one another. Love keeps creativity humane. Creativity keeps coherence alive. Coherence keeps Love from collapsing under pressure.

Together, they form a way of life that doesn't depend on control, certainty, or perfection. This is what Radical Wholeness looks like when it's no longer an intervention.

It's how you live to meet the moment. How you participate without fragmenting?

And while this doesn't solve the world's problems, it changes how you show up to them.

Over time, something in you settles.

The constant pressure to brace, correct, or prove begins to fall away. You feel it first in the body, a softening of the jaw, a breath that reaches further down, a little more room inside your own chest. The world has not become simpler, but you are no longer meeting it from strain.

From this place, you stop reinforcing the very patterns that once shaped you. Not through effort or vigilance, but because there is no longer an internal fracture asking to be managed. Complexity can be held without flattening it. Differences can be met without defense.

What you offer now is quieter, but more trustworthy, because it is no longer authored by effort, fear, or identity, but sourced through coherence with the same intelligence that animates life itself.

This is what it means to live as a coherent system, faithful to love, faithful to creation, and available to the moment.

In a world under real strain, this way of being matters. Not as a role, or a stance, or an identity, but as a lived orientation that does not add harm to what is already breaking and does not turn away from what still wants to be met.

## Inquiries

- Where do you notice Love, creativity, and coherence beginning to move together in your life?

- What changes when Radical Wholeness becomes orientation rather than effort?

- How does your participation in the world shift when you trust yourself as a coherent system?

# Author Biography

Holly Woods, PhD, is the founder of Emergence Institute and creator of the Living Portal™ Initiation and its CosmoSync™ Methods, a groundbreaking approach to human coherence that integrates developmental psychology, trauma healing, subtle-energy science, cosmology, and evolutionary theory. With four decades of experience as a coach, mentor, and researcher, Holly guides visionaries, leaders, and seekers into Radical Wholeness, purpose alignment, and embodied creative expression.

Her work combines Parts Alchemy, quantum field awareness, somatic coherence, and mythic cosmology into a unified development path for the future human. She is the author of The Golden Thread: Where to Find Purpose in the Stages of Your Life, and the publisher of Living Portal Press, a home for forward-thinking works on consciousness, coherence, and evolution.

Holly lives and teaches at the threshold where psyche, Earth, and Cosmos converge—helping people remember who they truly are, why they are here, and how to live as coherence embodied.

# Use of AI

Parts of this manuscript were developed in dialogue with AI language models, which were used to support idea exploration. All AI-generated content was reviewed, edited, and integrated by the author to ensure accuracy, coherence, and alignment with the intended meaning. The conceptual framing, structure, arguments, and all final editorial decisions are entirely the work of the author, with AI serving as a creative and analytical tool—much like a research assistant or editorial partner. Full responsibility for the content rests with the author.